MW01281919

Life

WE ARE IN THIS TOGETHER

Arthenia Newburn

ISBN 978-1-65435-122-9 (Paperback)

Copyright © 2017 by Arthenia Newburn
All rights reserved. No part of this publication may be
reproduced, distributed, or transmitted in any form or by any
means, including photocopying, recording, or other electronic or
mechanical methods without the prior written permission of the
publisher. For permission requests, solicit the publisher via the
address below.

Arthenia Newburn Ministries
724 Harrison Ave
Rockford, IL 61104
www.arthenianewburn.org

Printed in the United States of America

ACKNOWLEDGMENTS

First of all, I thank God for my salvation. I thank Him for the privilege of being able to do what He has called me to do and especially for Him pushing me to write this book. And I thank Him for guiding me from the start to the finish.

I appreciate my husband of thirty-eight years, Dr. Kerry L. Newburn, who is the love of my life. For his patience with me while writing this book, I am grateful!

I want to thank my sons, Timothy, Devolis, and Demond, godsons, Ronald and Dustin, goddaughter, Perginia, and friends, Sandra and Janice, for their encouragement and for their having helped me to stay motivated to do all that God has called me to. To my daughter Brandi and to all of my grandchildren, who are always in my heart.

I am thankful for my parents, Ethel Fay and Harvey Hammock, Gloria Gene Young, and the late Arthur E. Young, for their prayers, and never ending love. I am also thankful for my siblings, Ricky, Steve, and the late Phillip E. Young who I was raised up with. Linda, Terry, Falesha, and all of my nieces and nephews, and special cousin, Kenneth.

A very special thank you to the late Mother Frances Daugherty for her commitment to Christian education, and to the late Dr. Clayborn Salter for his wisdom and integrity. And to my aunt, Adnita Thompson, who is a great educator. They each have inspired me tremendously. And to all of my friends and sisters in the Lord who have supported me in many ways.

Last, but certainly not least, to my beloved Bethel Missionary Baptist Church family, a big thank you! For the greatest support and love given that anyone could give to a pastor and his family. For your kindness and care for us, thank you! It will never be forgotten.

Great appreciation to Maxine Rhyne and Nina Kelly for all of their hard work and care that they have extended to me.

INTRODUCTION

This book is written to enlighten, encourage, and help non-believers as well as believers everywhere and in every walk of life. To challenge the body of Christ, to be the body of Christ at all times! To live and model the life ofsJesu attitude, behavior, and conduct.

Remembering to call ourselves in check when needed. The people of God must realize the need to check themselves, so that there will be no need for others to call them in check.

I want to remind the church that Christ died for our sins, not giving us a license to sin but giving us the right or reason not sin (practice sinning). He is not going to come down and force any of us to do what is right.

We are called to strive for perfection as Christ our model for life and living is perfect. And with the help of the Holy Spirit, we are capable of living such a life. We must live our lives out in ways that are pleasing to the Lord. A life that is holy, righteous, consecrated, and yielded unto God. And for the church, it's still right!

This is so necessary today because of those who do not understand the grace of God and what it did for us. It is the free and unmerited love and favor of God toward us or given to us. The Lord said to me some years ago, "Jesus Christ is grace!" Christ and all that he has done for the world was God giving His grace to the world. Jesus was full of grace and truth.

Because of grace, we (the church) should have no desire whatsoever to live an unholy lifestyle. We should never receive the grace of God as a pass to sin. Yes, we are covered by the blood of Jesus, but there are still consequences for sin.

Jesus is the head of the church, the sinless son of God, who has called us to be like him. With this in mind, it is imperative that we allow him to stretch us spiritually. We need not to try and stretch ourselves, for to do that apart from the Lord is failure. With Him, by Him, and through Him, we can accomplish and achieve anything He has assigned us to or that He has ordained for our lives. But without Him, we can do nothing!

He is our help. The spirit of God who resides in us is our helper. So no more excuses for living careless, raggedly, ungodly lives. With His help, we can do and be better.

CHAPTER 1

Walk with God

We are in this together! These are the words that I heard as I was going through what I thought was a normal day in my life. After hearing this, the Lord began to minister to me. He revealed to me that *it is not*, nor has it ever been His will for man (mankind) to go through life or live life apart from Him. He created man to walk with Him!

We often say, and have heard others say, "I want or need the Lord to walk with me every day." But God is saying, "Walk with me every day! Let me take the lead, let me tell you which direction to go in, where to go. Let me guide you to the job that I have for you. Allow me to send you to the right city, the perfect place that I have ordained for you to be."

But today it seems as if men are trying to talk God into walking with them in the direction that they choose to go in not realizing that we are in partnership in life with God and He is the senior partner! So what we desire or will in life does n ot supersede what He desires or will for us in life.

We can go through this life trying to operate on our own and settling for less than God's best for our lives, or we can walk with God and let him help us to have His best. It is never good to do anything apart from Him, without seeking His help, counsel, guidance, and His protection. Whether it is a decision that has to be made right now or later, make it with God! He knows what is best for you.

Should I date? Who should I date? Should I marry? Who should I marry? Do I get this house or that house? Do I rent it or buy it? Do I move or do I stay here? Should I join this church or that church? What city? Which job? Which college? Should I purchase a car at this time or should I wait? There is a big question mark behind each of these decisions because we really aren't sure what is best for us. The Lord already knows the answers to every one of these questions and all others. If you will walk with Him, He will lead and guide you in every area of life.

When God Seems Silent

What do you do when you have heard the voice of God, when you have been obedient to God? And in the midst of your being obedient or following his instructions, God seems to get quiet on you or He seems to stop talking to you? This can be so puzzling and even scary. You might ask, "God, why are you so silent now when I really need to hear from you? I'm waiting for you to tell me what to do next." And it still seems as though no answer comes. What do you do? You pull from your spirit what you know! You know that you do know God and He is your heavenly Father. He is faithful, loving, and kind. You also know that He is always on time!

You know that the Lord knows where you are at this time in your life. You know that He has kept you up until this present time and He will continue to keep and lead you to the place where He intends for you to be. You know, believe, and receive the word of God. The Lord said, "I will answer you when you call and show you great and mighty things, which you know not" (Jeremiah 33:3).

The Kingdom of God has come to you as it is in heaven. Whatever heaven has, you have on earth (Matthew 6:10). Jesus has already made this provision for you, the believer. All of your provisions for life come from God. He may send them through many different means, vessels, or various avenues, but He is the source. By faith, just know that He has not forgotten you. He is in fact still speaking to you and still moving on your behalf.

Continue to love on Jesus, who is not only your Savior and Lord but He is your everything. Everything that you have ever needed or will ever need, you will find it in Him.

What do you do when it seems as though God is not saying anything or doing anything? Believe! Believe! Believe! You are of the seed of Abraham and you have the faith of your spiritual father. "Therefore it is of faith, that it might be by grace; to the end the promise might be sure to all the seed; not to that only to which is of the law, but to that also which is of the faith of Abraham; who is the father of us all" (Romans 4:16). Therefore, stagger not at the promise of God through unbelief but be strong in faith, giving glory to God. Be fully persuaded that what He has promised He is also able to perform.

Follow His Lead

He promised, if you would not lean unto your own understanding, but trust in Him with all of your heart. And in all of your ways, acknowledge Him. He will direct your paths. Look at the partnership. We acknowledge and He directs. And we move only as He directs. Somewhat like a play or a Broadway show where God is the director, we are the cast, and the whole world is the audience. And if we follow the director's lead, all will see us at our best. But if the cast does not work with the director, the production will be a blunder. Likewise with the people of God. When we refuse to allow Him to direct us, we end up making blunders in our lives.

When I was a girl growing up in Arkansas, we used to play a game called "Follow the Leader." You had to go wherever the head person, or "leader" we called them, would take you and do whatever the leader did. To follow the Lord in such a way would prevent us from making stupid mistakes as we go through life.

In Every Area

The Lord wants to teach us how to be loving mates, because we really are not able to love right in our marriages until we learn to love like God loves. His love is real, genuine, and unconditional. He wants to show us how to be caring parents, good grandparents, kind neighbors, and excellent employees. Even if you are single, have no children, unemployed, and live in an isolated area, God will meet you where you are. His desire is for you to partner in life with Him, and for you to allow Him to take the lead.

"Where He Leads Me, I Will Follow" was an old gospel hymn that used to be sung periodically in our services on Sundays, and how befitting it was for the church then. We would do well to implement hymns like this one, back into our service.

CHAPTER 2

Faith in God and His Ability

In the church today, there is a misconception concerning faith. Faith is a gift from God. The Bible tells us that faith is the assurance of the things we hope for, being the proof of things we do not see and the conviction of their reality. Many in the body of Christ are not operating in the faith at all mainly because their faith is in themselves or in their faith "faith in faith" I call it, which does not produce anything. We are told by Jesus, "Have faith in God (Mark 11:22)," not faith in what you strongly feel will happen. Faith is not predicated on what you feel. It is a belief and trust in God and His ability to do. Even when He works in and through you, it is God who does the work. Therefore, you should always look to Him with expectation.

What do I mean by this? If you are asking, you must look to God to do what He said in His word that He would do. The Lord said to Jeremiah, "For I will hasten my word to perform it"

(Jeremiah 1:12b). He was, and is, saying He will literally watch over His word to make sure that it is done. Therefore, you can expect that it will be.

Operating in faith is not having faith in your ability to fast and pray as some believe. You should implement both of these in your life as a Christian, but it is still faith in God and His ability, along with these, that work.

Too often there are those who have faith in what they believe and their belief is not in God, nor what he has said in His word. But when we line up with Him and His word, we can have what we are believing for.

The Lord taught me something about faith through His word and through application as well. "But wilt thou know, O vain man, that faith without works is dead?" (James 2:20) So there is something that we have to do as we continue to live this Christian life.

I am disturbed when some gives the indication that one does not have to put forth a great effort to live a saved life. They may not mean it like it sounds, but the effects are real. Many are falling by the wayside and away from the church as a result of no great effort being put into living a saved life. If there is no great effort on our part, we give God nothing to work with. And on the contrary, we give the enemy something to work with in our lives.

A Real Event

I had a real personal experience around 1990 where I operated in faith and the result just mesmerized me. I had been attending a class that was being given at a local church for the week. I was excited about the class because the instructor who taught it taught Greek also. I had planned to be there every night even with a husband, two young children, a dog, cooking, laundry, and cleaning, not to mention errands that had to be run during the week. Well one evening after supper, I went in and dressed for class. As I was getting ready to leave the house, a bad hailstorm mixed with rain came up, one of the worse that I had ever seen before. On the news the next day, it was reported that the hail was as large as golf balls and had damaged many cars at the car dealerships in the area. But at that time, I did not know. So being determined to make it to class on time, I grabbed a brown paper bag to hold over my head and proceeded to go out the door and get into the truck with my husband saying to me, "You need to wait until it lets up before you go out there."

And me replying, "I have to be on time for class." I didn't want to miss anything, so I kept going. I drove only a couple of blocks to get to the church and sat there in the parking lot praying, "Lord, please let this storm let up so I can go inside the church." I continued to sit there believing that God would let it slack up when I heard the Holy Spirit, like a loud voice inside of me, say, "Faith without work is dead." And I automatically knew what He was telling me. I was praying, but I was still sit - ting there in the truck. I had not moved, not even a finger. But immediately after I heard Him, I put my hand on the handle of the door, opened it, and stepped out into the storm. After I stepped out and began to move toward the church, before I could take two steps forward, I realized that everything had stopped.

But what I was most fascinated by was I looked around, believing that God had done that just because I had asked in faith and because I did what He told me to do. He revealed to me His ability to do. It became even more miraculous. I looked across from the church's parking lot. The storm was still there. It looked like a curtain of hard rain and hail falling. Cars on the street were going into it and coming through it. It was one of the most amazing sights that I had ever witnessed. The excitement in my spirit, at that point, caused me to dance a little dance right there in the parking lot. I vowed not to say or tell anyone about what happened, but when I got inside the church and in my class, I whispered to one of the ladies, "You won't believe what just happened when I arrived in the parking lot." I had to tell somebody!

I've seen God do so many things, but that was an awesome display of what faith in God and His ability can manifest.

As a believer, your faith in God brings great glory and honor to Him. And the Lord still honors faith that is directed toward Him.

CHAPTER 3

Peace, Peace

In the world, there is an absence of peace in the minds and hearts of men and not in the secular world only. Men and women everywhere, even in church, struggle with having peace in their lives.

With the breakdown of the family in our society, with the economy still unstable, with the job situations still being in array, with a lack of finances, high mortgages, insurance payments, medical bills, tuition fees, and with just the basic of living, it's not surprising to find out that there is unrest in the lives of people now.

However, for the believer, there is no need to go through life without peace. We have been assured the peace of Christ! "Peace I leave with you, my peace I give unto you: not as the world giveth, I give unto you. Let not your heart be troubled, neither let it be afraid (John 14:27). In the world, there will always be some kind of trouble or problems, but remember the words of Christ, 'that in me ye might have peace.' In the world ye shall have tribulations: but be of good cheer; I have overcome the world" (John 16:33).

Yes, we have a peace within us, which allows us to remain calm when the world turns chaotic. I receive great comfort in remembering, as well as saying what Isaiah said, "Thou wilt keep Him in perfect peace, whose mind is stayed on thee: because he trusteth in thee" (Isaiah 26:3). What Isaiah was saying is that the Lord will keep us in inward peace, outward peace, in peace with God, and peace in all situations in life. When we keep our minds on God and the things of God instead of the world and the things of the world, we will have perfect peace. The peace that God gives, we could never obtain on our own. Temporary peace you may be able to get every now and then, but lasting peace comes from Him. Philippians 4:7 says, "It's a peace which surpasses all understanding, and it will guard your hearts and your minds in Christ Jesus."

We can be encouraged through the words of our Lord, "Now the Lord of Peace himself give you peace always by all means. The Lord be with you all" (2 Thessalonians 3:16). And we need Him! Because of the confusion even in our churches at times, the fights, the church splits, and because of the level of disrespect that is displayed among the people of God. We are called to live peaceably with one another. The Lord can help us to do that.

Peace among One Another

I was preparing for a conference a few years ago and the Lord spoke to me and said, "Write a declaration for the women and have them to read it out loud. In doing so, they will have a greater bond with one another. They will have a greater respect and appreciation for each other. This will help them to not be envious or jealous of one another." So I began to write what I called "A Sincere Declaration," and this is the content of it, "You are my sister, and I love you in the Lord. I'll pray for you every time I think of you. I'll encourage you as you go on your way. I will never be envious of what God is doing in your life. I'll bless God for the works that you do. And I'll thank God for using you in a unique way. For you are my sister in the Lord."

As it is my prayer that men, as well as women, will read in this book. I am revising this declaration for the whole church. "You are my brother, you are my sister, and I love you in the Lord. I'll pray for you every time I think of you. I'll encourage you as you go on your way. I'll never be envious of what God is doing in your life. I'll bless God for the works that you do. And I'll thank God for using you in a unique way. For you are my brother and you are my sister in the Lord." I am sharing this because I believe that it can and will help to promote peace among those in the body of Christ, if it is received. But if others refuse to live peaceably with you, just continue to let the peace of God rest within your heart. In doing so, you will exemplify Christ in your life.

I feel that it is necessary for me to tell you that you should not allow anyone to take your peace. The Lord is the one who gave it to you and He should be the only one who can take it from you.

The enemy will use anyone and anything that he can to cause you to lose the peace of God. So be on guard, stay alert spiritually, reject any and everything that disturbs your peace. Hold on to what God has given you.

CHAPTER 4

When Grief Comes

On the morning of May 11, 2005, I received a phone call from my mother. My husband, Kerry, had answered the call. Then shortly afterward, he brought the phone into the bedroom where I was. While still in the bed, I reached for it and said, "Hello," and all I could hear was my mother's voice in a frantic tone saying, "Cis, they killed my baby, he's gone." I replied, "Who, Momma?" because at that time, I had three brothers living who my mother had given birth to and this was her oldest of the four children.

She replied, "Phil, he's dead, he's gone! They let my baby die up there. I need you to come home, I need you to come home now." I said, "I'm coming," and after we talked for a few minutes, I mashed the button to turn the phone off. Then I rolled over on the bed and began to cry as though someone had beaten me down. My heart was so heavy, I was so full. I felt broken down, hurt and lost. At that moment, I didn't know what to do. I could not pray right then. All I could do at that time was just cry. I couldn't even get out the bed, I literally felt that weak.

My brother, Phil, had been arrested for committing a violent act during a nervous breakdown. Some refer to it as a mental breakdown. We knew that what he did was wrong. But while he was in jail, those who were in charge did not give him the proper care that he needed. After suffering from severe pain in his legs and body, he called my mother from jail to ask her for help because he was hurting bad. That was the last time that she heard from him.

They had taken him to the hospital that day, but brought him back to the jail. My mother called the jail requesting that they do more and get him additional help. She was asked in a rude way to stop calling, "We can do more for him than you can," was what she was told. Phil died later from a massive heart attack. He had blood clots in his legs that traveled to his heart.

Feeling So Alone

When I did get up from my bed, I immediately began to prepare to go from Illinois to our home state of Arkansas. My husband booked me a flight right away and drove me to the airport. Hours after receiving the call, I still felt so alone and weak. But as I sat in the airport waiting for my flight to leave, I began to pray and I took my little purse-sized Bible out and started to read it. While reading, I could hear God! He encouraged me so in His word that day. It was as though He stood up inside of me, and I had strength that I knew came from Him.

I asked Him to hold me, because I really wanted to run. But I knew if I took off running inside the airport, someone might call those people with the straightjackets to come and get me. So I sat there, with tears of gratitude in my eyes, and a heart filled with love and appreciation to God for being with me. He carried me through. And I was able to minister to the rest of my family during that period and in the days ahead. If the Lord had not been there with me, I never would have made it through that!

Some have said the loss of a sibling is harder than the loss of a parent. I've lost both sets of grandparents and a father. The level of grief that I experienced with my brother was almost devastating. Siblings grow up together and, I believe, this is the reason why we seem to hurt more.

Though I miss Phil tremendously, I know that I'll be reuniting with him some day. I am reminded of an article that I was inspired to write after the passing of a beautiful Christian woman in our community. In it, I shared a story that is recorded in 2 Samuel, the twelfth chapter, of King David and a child that he had. When you look closely at verses fifteen to twenty-three, you will find that the child became very sick. David besought God on behalf of the child. He fasted (would not eat), he lay all night upon the ground, before the Lord (he humbled himself before the Lord).

The elders of the house went to David to raise him up from the ground. But he would not get up. He stayed there. Neither did he eat bread with them (he continued fasting and seeking God).

After several days, the child died and the servants of David were afraid to tell him that the child died because they felt that while the child was yet alive, David would not hear them when they spoke unto him. They feared and questioned what he might do to himself once he found out that his child was dead.

When David saw that his servants whispered, he perceived the child was dead. So he asked his servants if the child was dead. They answered clearly, "He is dead." Then David rose from the ground and from praying for the child to live. Then, and only then, did he stop seeking God's intervention. He washed and anointed himself, changed his clothes, and went into the house of the Lord, and worshipped. Then he went to his own house and he asked for food to eat.

Because of David rising up and going on with his life, doing what he would normally do, his servants were confused. So they asked him, "What did you do and what are you doing?" They pointed out to him that they noticed, while his child was alive, he fasted and wept for it. And when the child died, he rose up and ate.

David's response to his servants was, "While the child was yet alive, I fasted and wept for I said, 'Who can tell whether God will be gracious to me that the child may live?' But now he is dead, wherefore should I fast? Can I bring him back again? I shall go to him, but he shall not return to me" (2 Samuel 12:22–23).

When those whom we love are sick, and yet alive, we are to do all that we can, praying that God will be gracious to us and allow them to live. But if he chooses to call them home, we can be comforted and have confidence in knowing that we will one day go to be with them.

God gave a great revelation through David concerning the resurrection of the dead. He revealed it to Job as well. Job said, "For I know that my Redeemer liveth, and that he shall stand at the latter day upon the earth: and though after my skin worms destroy this body, yet in my flesh shall I see God" (Job 19:25–26). The Lord also, through the apostle Paul, reassured us of the blessed hope of the resurrection. It is recorded, "For the Lord himself shall descent from heaven with a shout, with the voice of the archangel, and with the trump of God: and the dead in Christ shall rise first: Then we which are alive and remain shall be caught up together with them in the clouds, to meet the Lord in the air: and so shall we ever be with the Lord" (1 Thessalonians 4:16, 17).

As believers, we trust in and believe the word of God. We cannot bring our loved ones back, but we can most certainly prepare to one day be reunited with them. And until that time comes, we must go on with life on this side to fulfill the purpose and plan of God for our lives. Run on until we hear Him say, "Well done!"

CHAPTER 5

My Best Friend

In every season of life, we have different needs. Have you ever needed a friend close, someone to be right there in your corner? Someone who knows and understands you. Do you desire someone to be in your life who can and will help you out when you really need help? One who you can confide in and you'll never hear it again. Someone who will always be truthful. A friend who will be a friend for life.

I have a friend like that, one who is far greater even. He has all of these qualities and more. He is my best friend, the Holy Spirit, who is the spirit of God who lives in me. And as a matter of fact, He is God in me! And He is more real to me than anyone else in my life. I talk to Him about anything and He talks to me, especially during times when I desperately need to hear from God. I can be in the midst of a crowd and still hear Him. I don't hear Him clearly all the time but, at most, I am able to distinguish His voice from the voices of others around me.

When He speaks, it is always what the Lord would have Him to say, "For he shall not speak of himself; but whatsoever he shall hear; that shall he speak" (John 16:13b). Jesus taught that "the sheep know his voice, and they know not the voice of strangers" (John 10:4, 5).

To have a friend who you talk with every day, for weeks, months, and even years, almost always you recognize their voice, and it doesn't matter where you are. If you're in the grocery store and hear their voice a few aisle over, you know that Mary Ann, Sue, Bob, George, Greg, Beth, or whoever your friend is, you recognize that they are there by their voice.

We can become so tuned in to the voice of God to the point that wherever and whenever He speaks, we hear Him.

The Spirit Spoke to Me

As a child, I can recall hearing the Holy Spirit but I did not know who He was. When I was as young as ten years old, I remember being told that a childhood friend in Texarkana, Texas had died. "One of the twins died," was what I heard. Just a little while later, as I was playing outside in the yard, my mother called me to the door and shared with me that my grandmother called to let us know that one of the twin girls that I played with and spent time with when I would visit my grandmother had drowned. I was so sad when I heard it, and I didn't tell anyone that a voice had already told me.

Some years had passed and during those years, I had begun to spend quite a bit of time talking to God when I was alone, which was often because at that time I was an introvert and a loner.

When I was sixteen years old, I was in a service on a Saturday night at the St. Thomas Baptist Church in Hot Springs, Arkansas. While sitting there with my mother and her friend listening to a group sing whom I had never seen nor heard before, I noticed a young man singing with the group who was the same complexion as my grandfather. I heard the Lord say to me, "You're going to marry him." I sat there very still realizing what I had just heard, and then slowly I turned to my mother who was sitting to my left of me and said, "Momma, see that man down there? I'm going to marry him!" I did not explain it all to her. She took her hand and patted me gently on my thigh, and didn't say a word. Nothing more was said about it. We left before the service was over.

On Monday night, I was at my part-time job, which was a dairy/food joint, when three young men came in, the one I recognized right away as the same young man whom the Lord had spoken to me about at the church on that Saturday night. They sat down at a table and when I went out to take their orders, the same young man asked me if he could have my phone number. Neither of the other two asked, but that young man did. I said, "No," but later wrote it down and put it under the bread basket. He called me later that night and the rest was history. He and I have been married for thirty-eight years now. To God be the glory!

He Knows Everything

One Sunday, after the morning worship service at Bethel Baptist Church was ending and we had taken in those who wanted to be a member of the church, one of the deaconess and myself took a woman down to (what we call the Deacon's Room) to welcome her to the church, to let her know what was available at the church, and to pray with her. After getting the information we needed and sharing with her, I started to pray. While praying, the Holy Spirit said to me, "That's not a woman. It's a man. Look at his hands, look at his feet." I heard it just as clear as any other time that I've heard the Lord's voice. So when I said, "Amen," and opened my eyes, I looked at his hands. The fingers were thick. I looked at his feet and they were very thick. I said nothing about what I heard until I got in the truck with my husband who was the pastor.

I shared with him what I heard the Holy Spirit say. He said, "Oh, sista." I replied, "I know when I hear God." Well, I gazed out of the window, and said no more!

After a year or so had passed, one of the deaconess was asked to give this same lady a ride to the shelter. And she did, but the women's shelter would not allow her to stay. The deaconess, being frustrated by it, went in to inquire as to why when they had room for her. She was told, "Ma'am, we cannot allow him to stay here, that's a man." The Deaconess came immediately back to the church after dropping him off at another place. She drove up to where I was standing, got out of the car, and told me what had happened. I said to her, "Come with me, I want you to tell pastor."

The Holy Spirit does not lie. "But the anointing that ye have received of him abideth in you, and ye need not that any man teach you: but as the same anointing teacheth you of all things, and is truth, and is no lie, and even as it hath taught you, ye shall abide in him" (1 John 2:27). He is the spirit of truth, "Howbeit when he, the Spirit of truth, is come, he will guide you into all truth" (John 16:13a).

We love all men and will that all be saved. As believers, we do embrace all men but do not embrace all lifestyles. God love truth and He exposes that which is not truth.

There have been many times over the years that the Holy Spirit has spoken to me, giving me information concerning others, directed me to a certain person and to places. On one occasion, I was in a fairly new city we had not been there long at all. I wanted to purchase some fish to cook for dinner, so I asked around and someone told me about a fish market in a certain area of the city. So I got in my car and set out to find it. I drove up and down that area but could not see anything that resembled a fish market. So after searching for a while, I gave up.

I told the Holy Spirit I was going to go down the street one more time, and I was going to go home if I didn't see it.

I went up the street, turned around, and came back down. I saw nothing, so I turned into a place to turn around for home. I said, "Okay, Holy Spirit, I'm going home now." I put my car in reverse and as I got ready to back up, I noticed a sign on the side of the building that I had just pulled into to turn around and it was the fish market.

The Holy Spirit does know everything, He truly does. And I trust Him!

He Shows Me Visions

On the night that God called me in (saved me) and I accepted Jesus Christ as my savior, the Holy Spirit revealed to me seemingly all the wrong that I have ever done in my life.

With deep sorrow and great remorse in my heart, I began to weep. And as I was weeping and crying out, "I'm sorry, God. I love you, God. I love you, Jesus. I love you, Jesus." And all the time that I was crying out to Him, I could feel His love for me. And that prompted me to continue telling Him I was sorry for all the wrong that I had done and that I love Him.

It was as if someone had taken an old projector with a movie on it of my life and played or showed it on a screen, and I was watching. But all that was being shown was the wrong that I had done in my life. And all I could say repeatedly was, "I'm sorry, God. I love you, God. I love you, Lord. I love you, Jesus."

Knowing that God loved me like He did when I had been so wrong in my life, I was broken. I felt like I hurt God's heart.

And to this day, as a result of the change within me, I still do not want to hurt His heart.

I am grateful that the Holy Spirit showed me in a vision how undone and unfit I was for the Kingdom of God. For Him helping me to know that I was a sinner. I had sinned against God and needed my sins forgiven in order to live a saved life and to be able to live eternally with the Lord when I die.

In 1978, I was taking a bath and had a vision while sitting in the tub. Once again, it was as if I was watching a movie. I was consoling, who I thought was my mother, but I could not see absolutely clear as to who it was. In the vision, I was telling her that she had three children left, which were living, so she was still blessed. And then the vision went away.

I assumed that it was my mom. So I phoned Momma and shared with her what I had seen, and that I thought it was her in the vision. I asked her to tell my brothers, who were young men at the time, to lay low, to not go out that weekend, stay close to home. I was hoping that I might be able to help prevent the loss of either one of their lives.

Having forgotten that my mother-in-law had four children as well, I did not consider that it may have been her in the vision.

The very next day around the same time, I was bathing for the day as I normally did at that hour and the phone rang. In those days, the phone would continue to ring if the caller did not hang up. I got out of the tub, grabbed my towel, wrapped it around me, and hurried to the phone, which was in the living room. I picked the receiver up and answered.

It was my husband calling from work to tell me that his youngest brother, Cornell, had died and he would be driving home to get me so that we could go to his mother's house. After hanging the phone up, I realized who it was that I was consoling in the vision that I had. My heart was saddened and heavy for my husband's parents and for him also. As soon as possible, we went over and remained there at my mother-in-law's side, comforting her and other family members while relying on the Lord for our strength.

I have heard it said by loved ones of my own who were and are older, "The Lord won't let nothing sneak up on you." I have found it to be a true saying. The Holy Spirit is amazing! When He is at work, I am in awe. He has revealed hidden dangers, bad spirits, or evil spirits. He has exposed underhanded dealings. He has spoken life and pregnancy through me into the lives of several women that I know who were barren. He allowed me to see the inside of my house that I'm living in now for twenty-three years before I even moved to this city. He's amazing! What I appreciate most about Him is He teaches me how to live the Christian life and how to help others to do the same.

CHAPTER 6

Walking in Forgiveness

My heart was saddened as God began to have me to look at the church, His body, and how so many have chosen to walk in unforgiveness when He has commanded His children to forgive offenses. Some think that to forgive a person it means that they have to continue to allow that person to violate them, but this is not true! It does not mean that you have to continue to allow them to violate you, but to truly forgive. It does mean that you must treat one as though they never violated you. This is God's way! The Lord said in Matthew 6:12, "When we pray, we should ask him to forgive us our debts, as we forgive our debtors."

He also said in verses fourteen and fifteen, "That if we forgive men their trespasses, He will forgive us. But if we do forgive others, neither will our heavenly Father forgive us." I add to how Matthew Henry's commentary explained these passages. We must forgive as we hope to be forgiven, and therefore we must not only bear no malice, nor revenge. We must not rebuke or criticize our brother or sister with the injuries he or she has done us, nor rejoice in any hurt that befalls him or her. But we must be ready to help them and do them good. Those who would have mercy with God must show mercies to others!

Let me remind the people of God that we are not to conform to the world and its ways, but we are called to be transformed (changed) by the renewing of our mind. And we renew our minds with the word of God and time spent in the Lord's presence.

Choosing not to forgive others is like one taking a bottle of poison and sipping on it until he/she dies. Choose to live and be blessed. Forgive! As we sincerely think about how much God loves us and how much He has forgiven us of. Who are we to not forgive others?

God has called His children to forgive, and to walk in love with all men. And if we desire to live and have the blessed life that the Lord has for us, we must obey Him fully! Remembering that we are called to represent God well on the earth. And the Lord will bless and keep us as we endeavor to do His will.

Let It Go

Often in life, people tend to hold on to offenses. Wrong that has been done to them or against them. Sometimes, even unknowingly, they hang on to things that they should let go of. Some might say, "You don't understand. He hurt me." Forgive and let it go! "But I gave that man everything." Forgive and let it go! "But I was just a little girl when it happened." Forgive and let it go! "They did not apologize for what they did." Forgive and let it go! "But I was treated so badly." Forgive and let it go! "They continue to look over me." Forgive and let it go.

Let me share a true story with you. There was a man who was so loving, caring, and kind, who lived in a beautiful area with his father. One day, they made the decision that he (the son) would leave their residence and go to another place to live for a while. So he moved into a place where many of the people who lived around him were not like him. In fact, some of them were just cruel! But that did not stop him from being who he was. This man did so much good while he was in this place. He showed great compassion and was helpful to others everywhere that he went.

Well, after a certain period had passed, jealousy, envy, and strife had filled the hearts of some of the people who did not want this man doing the things that he did. And right about the same time, the man had received word from his father that it was time for him to return home.

But before he left, some of the people in that area had planned and plotted to kill him. This plan was already in motion. They had him arrested with fake charges against him. They sentenced him to die. They took his clothes off. They spit on him. They beat him, hitting him over and over until pieces of his flesh began to come off with each strike. They laughed and made fun of him. And when they were done or finished bruising him, they nailed his body on a tree, stood the tree up, and left him hanging there to die. But before he died, he looked down at those who had caused him so much grief, sorrow, and pain, and he said, "I let it go!"

If you do not know, Christ Jesus is the man in this story. When we were separated from God, because of our sinful nature, He sent his son to suffer and die to bring us back in fellowship with himself. In doing so, Christ endured great per-secution from those who had hated Him, yet He let it go asking the Father to forgive them because they did not know what they were doing.

We can learn from His example, to pardon others for the wrong that they have done. Release the offense, release them, and release yourself. I say this, because too often people find themselves bound and not able to move forward in life, because they have not let go of the ill that was done to them. Don't become paralyzed by the offenses of others.

It's hard to trust again, if you never come to the realization that not all people are deceitful. It's a challenge to love again, when you've been abused and hurt by someone whom you loved. But choose to love again!

People struggle sometimes with being in new relationships because of past hurts and failures in a previous relationship. They tend to put a wall up, or they will refuse to give themselves fully in the new relationship. This is not good! And it should not be a pattern for believers. So get rid of the invisible wall, come out the box. You've been in your own little world long enough.

God Made Us to Soar

Some years ago, I remember waking up on a Saturday morning in Wisconsin where I was for a women's conference. I was the speaker for the morning session. After praying, as it is a good habit of mine every morning to play praise and worship music or to sing praise and worship songs, I began to sing the gospel song "I Believe I Can Fly." Then I went into the bathroom to brush my teeth. As I was brushing, and still humming the song with toothpaste in my mouth, I asked God to teach me how to fly. Immediately, I heard the Lord say, "You're already flying, I'm going to teach you how to soar."

I did not understand the difference between flying and soaring. He revealed to me that the Holy Ghost was going to take me higher than I could fly on my own, and that it would not take my effort for me to soar. If I would just get in the wind of the Holy Ghost, I would soar and He will take me where I need to go.

God reminded me that when an eagle, in his strength and power, fly so high he gets in the wind and just soars with no effort of his own. The wind allows him to soar gracefully from one place to another far above everything.

We were made to soar. We can rise above any and everything that has happened to us. Turn loose of whatever may be hindering or preventing you from soaring. God created us to soar.

CHAPTER 7

God Is Your Source

To look to any means other than God for life and living would be a great mistake. Our very existence and being is in Him.

Paul said, "It is in Him we live, move and have our being" (Acts 17:28). So we are not able to breathe, move, or do anything without Him. In Genesis 2:7, it was God who breathed into man the breath of life.

There are those who believe they are self-sufficient and do everything in their own might, strength, and power. But Jesus said, "For I am the vine, ye are the branches: he that abideth in me, and I in him, the same bring forth much fruit for without me you can do nothing" (John 15:5).

The truth is, we are helpless without the Lord. If we had to live this life without Him, we would be miserable. I said to God one time, "I don't know how men make it in this world without you, Lord." He replied, "They don't! They try to make it with drugs, alcohol, multiple relationships, sex, and whatever else they can do to get by." I understood His reply. To just get by in life is not making it!

Even gifts and talents all came from God. And He gives them to us as He sees fit. Therefore, they did not derive from our parents or grandparents. What they possessed came from God. He was their source as well. And their generations were quick to acknowledge where all of their blessings came from. Whether it was a personal gift or talent that they had, a new job, a new home, a family, good health, an education, spiritual growth, and whatever else they had. They knew that God provided it and they gave Him the glory.

I Am Jehovah-Jireh

There was a time in my life when I did not know, as I do today, the provision of God. Oh, I knew He was God and believed that there was nothing too hard for Him, but I did not realize that I do not have to worry about anything in life. The Lord said to me when I was a younger woman, and I have shared it with others for years now, "You either believe me or you don't, there is nothing in between."

I found out through experience that not only will the Lord make a way somehow, He has already made a way of provision for me in this world and for all of His children because He is no respect of person (Romans 2:11, Acts 10:34). This means God shows no partiality, whoever fears Him and works righteousness and is accepted by Him. And He will bless all of His children. He is a loving Father. Therefore all of His children receive the best care.

According to Genesis 22:14, the Lord's name is Provider, Jehovah-Jireh, "God who sees." In the RV, it shall be provided. Whatever you and I need, God has already taken care of.

I often think of what Jesus said concerning provision for life, "Therefore I say unto you, take no thought for your life, what ye shall eat, or what ye shall drink; nor yet for your body, what ye shall put on. Is not the life more than meat, and the body than raiment?"

Behold the fowls of the air: for they sow not, neither do they reap nor gather into barns; yet your Heavenly Father feedeth them. Are ye not much better than they?" (Matthew 6:25, 26)

Just recently, on our side porch up high on a wooden pole, a bird built a nest and laid three eggs in it. My husband and I did not touch it, nor did we remove it because of the eggs. We wanted to wait until they were hatched and out of the nest before removing it. I go out to the side porch at least once or twice a day. I stand out there just to get some fresh air in the mornings, and at other times I go out to put trash in the can, which is on the porch.

A few days ago, while standing at the door looking through the glass, I noticed the mother and how she was caring for these now three little birds that were around two weeks old. I quickly grabbed my cell phone so that I could get pictures of what I was seeing. As the three little ones reached their tiny beaks in the air when the mother flew to the nest, it was as if they knew she had something for them to eat even before they got it in their mouths. They would open and seemingly get excited about what was coming not having even received it yet. What caught my attention the most was I witnessed a principle that I often teach when I'm having Bible classes. "Expectation," we must have it in our lives. Those baby birds were expecting to be fed. They were solely relying on their mother to take care of them.

On several days, I watched the mother as she would go out in the yard to get food, fly up to her babies to feed them faithfully. As she provided for them, it was amazing to see the instinct that God had put in her. If I would open the side door, she would go away but came right back to them. Under her care, they grew and left the nest in what I thought was a short time.

We've had lots of rain here lately and a bad storm last week, but somehow the nest stayed in place and the momma and her babies were taken care of. That's God! If God looks out for and provides for birds, you know that He will take care of you.

Don't worry about protection or your needs being met in life. The Lord has you covered.

He shall cover thee with His feathers, and under His wings shalt thou trust: His truth shalt be thy shield and buckler (Psalms 91:4). So stop crying, don't fret any longer. Settle your nerves. Let expectation rise up inside of you. Continue to look to God knowing in your heart that He will provide. "But my God shall supply all your need according to His riches in glory by Christ Jesus" (Philippians 4:19).

I make this confession often, "If God could take care of a whole nation of people (Israel), when He brought them out of Egypt, and into the promise land, I know that He can and will take care of me and mine." And as a result of making it, I do not fret nor concern myself with how we're going to live from day to day. God has us covered!

Adorn the Inner Man

Our church was leaving on a bus trip once. My husband and I sat up front right behind the bus driver for that day. As I sat there, I was captivated by how beautifully dressed the women of our church were. They, one by one, stepped up into the bus.

During those days, our family did not have much, especially not a lot on finances. So I would not have been considered a well-dressed woman at all. And I was okay with that because it meant more to me for my husband, who was a pastor, and in the public's eye to look nice. That was more important than what I had on to me. Not to mention, I knew how to take what I had, wash it, tack it (if needed), and how to wear it. With the Lord's help, I've always known how to look presentable.

The members continued to board the bus and the women's fashionable outfits were still catching my attention.

Then I heard the Lord say, "First Peter 3:3." I said to Him, "Lord, I don't know what that is." So I reached down at my feet where I had my purse and my Bible. I picked the Bible up, turned to that passage, and began to read, "Whose adorning let it not be that outward adorning of plaiting the hair, and of wearing of gold, and of putting on of apparel." And I continued reading the next verse, which said, "But let it be the hidden man of the heart, in that which is not corruptible, even the ornament of a meek and quiet spirit which is in the sight of God of great price."

Shortly after reading it, and meditating on it, the Lord said to me, "Dress your inside, and I'll dress you on the outside." I was in my early twenties then, and to this day God has kept His word to me. I stayed in the word and in His presence growing spiritually, allowing Him to teach me how to adorn my inner man. While I was doing that, He was sending me everything that I needed to be well-dressed on the outside. And He still does!

Over the years, people have bought me clothes, suits, dresses, shoes, purses, hats, diamond earrings, necklaces, and even given me diamond rings a couple of times. They have bought me coats and seamstresses have made me clothes. My God has kept His word and I am truly grateful.

I can honestly say that most of my clothes have been purchased by others, who have allowed God to use them to be a blessing unto me. And it has always been my prayer that He would return unto them a hundred-fold blessing for their kindness and for their generosity.

To receive gifts from others used to be a great challenge for me. Because I always loved and enjoyed giving, I could not see myself receiving from people. I felt that I was the giver and there was no way that I could take anything from anyone other than family. That was pride! To be the recipient of gifts made me very uncomfortable at first, but the Lord helped me to understand that He blesses others through their giving just as He blesses me when I give gifts.

No one should go through life looking for others to give them something. To have your hand out to give to another is far better than having it out to receive. If you are giving, that means that you have something already and you are blessed. If you do not give or know how to be a blessing in the lives of others, you will never experience the fullness of God's blessings in your life. I thank God for unveiling this truth to many.

And I also thank Him for helping me to get rid of pride, and for Him teaching me how to receive from others in the right spirit.

CHAPTER 8

When Bad Things Happen

We have heard the question asked over and over again by many, "Why do bad things happen?" or "Why do bad things happen to good people?"

It is virtually impossible to answer this question. But because of life itself, or the occurrences in life, things happen. Bad things as well as good things.

God made this world and those in it, good! "And God saw everything that He had made, and, behold, it was very good" (Genesis 1:31a). But mankind, God's greatest creation, fell, causing sin to reign in the earth. It was in the Garden of Eden that man became wicked and began to do evil. Out of man's disobedience, sin was wroth. Jealousy, hatred, strife, murder, sexual immorality, stealing, robbing, abuse, and every other sinful act of man derived from the fall of man. Down through the generations, mankind, in his sinful state, has done and continued to do bad things. And unfortunately, there are those who became victims of their wrong doing.

When I was twelve years old, a friend of my mother's, who had two young children, needed someone to keep her little girls while she went out to a party. So she asked my mother if I could stay with them. Momma said, "No!" And I'm sure that she had her reasons for saying no but with much pleading and begging on my part, she changed her mind and consented. I was so adamant about doing it because I wanted to make some money of my own. I thought I would be able to buy some things that I wanted as a girl nearing her teen years. That was the primary reason for my being so determined to babysit that night.

Well that night came and I was there in the home of the friend. She told me how to care for the girls and when to put them to bed, then she left for her outing. Everything seemed okay and the night appeared to be like a normal night. After the girls were asleep and down, I laid down as well. And with everything seemingly calm, I fell asleep not realizing that my life was about to be altered, changed for the worse.

I was awoken by someone, a man, who had his hand over my mouth and threatened me as to what he would do if I made any noise and did not lie still. I did not know who he was and I feared what he was trying to do. I was just a young girl, scared, and crying, but that did not stop him from raping me. I realized that I was all alone, so I laid there helpless as a ruthless man took from me that which no person has a right to take from a child, their innocence!

After he was done, he left. And there I remained, afraid and hurt in my heart as well as in my body. I cried until I could not cry anymore, and, at the same time, I wondered why it happened to me. I did not understand how come God did not protect me. Not knowing at that time that He was trying to protect me by having Momma to say no, initially, when I asked if I could babysit. Of course, it was later in life when I received that revelation.

In tears, I shared this publicly with the world in hope that it will help others who have had bad things happen to them, to know that they are not alone. And to assure them that with the Lord's help, they can and will make it just as I have.

After the friend returned home, I told her what had happened. She took me to the hospital where my mother, having been called, met us. I was checked or examined by a physician. The police were brought in, a report was made, and then I was released to go home with my mom.

I cannot express the hurt and shame that I felt, but it was mild compared to the hurt, embarrassment, and shame that I would experience later.

I attended middle school during that time. On one afternoon, a couple of days later, us students were hanging out in an area that we stood around in after lunch period when a group of kids approached me. And the spokesman of the group asked me openly if I was the girl who got raped the other night. I did not know how they knew about it. Shocked and taken by surprise, I said, "No!" Then one of the other kids said, "Yes, it was you." I said nothing more. I just walked off from them. That was the beginning of a life filled with much shame and low self-esteem for me.

To feel dirty and different from others because of something that was done to you is hard, and it is enough to cause you to have low self-esteem. I stayed to myself mostly anyway but after that day at school, I really became a loner. I felt that no one knew what I was going through. I did not talk to anyone about it, so how could they know? Yet, in my attitude, I began to act out my frustration and anger because of what had happened to me.

I did not feel God's presence with me nor His love in my heart, which made me very sad because I believed that He loved and cared for me prior to what happened that night. And I loved Him.

What had happened was "I stopped liking me," as I called it. I did not love myself, so I felt that God no longer loved me. Those feelings remained for years until the Lord personally came to see about me, and I released everything to Him.

God took away all of the shame, the guilt, the hurt, the pain, the sadness, the brokenness, and the embarrassment. He let me know, in my heart, that I had done nothing wrong and that I had been done wrong. He gave me a tender heart, love, and a genuine concern for others.

As a result of having been deeply hurt in life, I have no desire to cause injuries nor harm to anyone intentionally. God has given me a great desire to want to bring healing to others who feel low and discarded in life. I want to let people know that God can wash you and leave you feeling completely new, as though you have never been touched. In this life, it is necessary for this to take place in order to freely give yourself to another, in the right way and in the right relationship.

Not being promiscuous, but to be able to allow someone to love you and for you to be able to express or give love back to them. And, *no*, the perpetrator was never caught or brought to justice.

Where Was God

Where was God? This is the question that is most frequently asked in the lives of those who have had bad things happen to them. And I certainly voiced the same at times. But I found out later, and I have come to know, that He was with me preventing the enemy from destroying me. I am positive that the bad, which has happened to me, was designed to destroy me. And it almost did. But God had a purpose and plan for my life that was far greater than my parents or I knew. And as I reflect back on it, and look at where He has brought me to, I cannot help but have praise in my belly. I'm leaping in my spirit, even as I write. Hallelujah! Glory! Glory! Glory to God!

Just as the Lord brought me through, He can bring you through. Do what I did, release it!

I decree, by the authority that has been given unto me, in the name of Jesus Christ of Nazareth, the son of the living God, whose I am and whose you are that you will no longer be bound by what has happened to you. In Jesus's name, you will not have a mental breakdown but you will break through. Sadness will no longer be your companion every day. I speak unto you the joy of the Lord, which is your strength. I assure you that God loves you and He is with you!

I pray that the Lord will reveal that He has always been with you, keeping the enemy from destroying your life. There is a reason that He has kept you alive also. It would be a wise move on your part to seek and pursue Him, to find out why.

In Esther 4:8-14, Mordechai told Esther (Hadassah) to go in unto the King, on behalf of the Jews, who were going to be destroyed by their enemy, Haman, who hated them. Mordechai knew that Esther could be killed also just for going in unto the King not summoned. But he believed that her life would be spared because she was perhaps raised up or kept for the very purpose of being in that place at that time to help her people, the Jews. Esther did go in unto the King and interceded on their behalf, and their lives were saved because of her. God kept Esther alive for a reason that even she knew not of.

For all of the little girls and young boys who have been raped. For all of the women, young or old, and men as well who have suffered abuse of any kind. For all of those who have been molested, beaten, neglected, and even tortured.

Just know that every perpetrator of a crime against another will have to give an account someday unto God, if not unto man, for the wrong, which they have done. The evil seed that they have sown, if not repented of, will bring forth a harvest into their lives or into the lives of their descendants.

"Keeping mercy for thousands, for giving iniquity and transgressions, and sin, and that will by no means clear the guilty; visiting the iniquity of the fathers upon the children, and upon the children's children, unto the third and to the fourth generations" (Exodus 34:7).

God will deal with those who wrong others. In Romans 12:19, He said, "We are not to avenge ourselves, because vengeance is His, and He will repay." So, clearly, God will handle those who have hurt us.

CHAPTER 9

Knowing Jesus Christ

There is life after this life here on Earth. I never take for granted that a person is saved. It is my desire to know, if possible, that they are. God has called me to be a soul winner for Christ.

He has put a burden in my heart to bring men to the knowledge of Christ Jesus so that they will know, without a doubt, when they die they will be with Him to live throughout eternity.

It's time to think about what will happen when you die. And we all will die on this side or on this earth, should Christ tarry. Where will you go? Where will you spend eternity? In heaven with God or in hell with Satan? You do have a choice, and the choice is only yours to make. The word of God says, "He that hath the Son, hath life; and he that hath not the Son of God hath not life" (1 John 5:12).

Is there a longing deep within you that you cannot explain? Does it feel as though something is missing in your life? Has your heart been broken and you do not know if anyone can help to heal it? Is your back up against a wall or perhaps you are in a situation where you see no way out? Has loneliness, helplessness, depression, and sadness consumed you?

There is help, there is hope, and there is a way out. His name is Jesus, the son of God. He is the savior of the world. Salvation comes through no other. "Neither is there salvation in any other; for there is none other name under heaven given among men, whereby we must be saved" (Acts 4:12). He is waiting for you to call unto Him. He will save you and deliver you from anything, including the hand of Satan.

Jesus loves you! He died on the cross for you to be able to live and have life more abundantly. "The thief cometh not, but for to steal, and to kill, and to destroy: I am come that they may have life and that they might have it more abundantly" (John 10:10). Matthew Henry says, "Life in abundance is eternal life, life without death or fear of death, life and much more."

There is nothing that you have done in your life that He will not forgive if you repent. Tell God that you are sorry for your sins and ask Jesus to come in and take control of your life. He will, but you must be willing to give Him control.

He will take only what we are willing to give Him. If you have done this, you are now saved. Start to know Christ better or more intimately by praying every day and reading the Bible daily. I recommend that you start by reading Matthew, Mark, Luke, John, and the book of Acts first. In these books, you get to know Christ Jesus and you are able to walk with Him as he walked when he was on the earth. This will make it easier for you to model His life here in your life. I pray that God will continue to bless and keep you!

Stay with God

Much has been said about whether or not a person can walk away from God. Some believe that if one is able to walk away from the faith, perhaps they never really had faith to begin wi th. Some people hold and believe that once saved, always saved, and that the grace of God can and will keep even those who choose to go back into the world or turn away from God.

I hold and believe that the grace of God will keep anyone who wants to be kept. I believe that God has given to all mankind a free will and that God himself will not violate that fre e will. Man can choose to live for God or not live for God. The Lord never has, nor will he ever force anyone to serve Him.

When David said in the book of Psalms that, "I will love thee, O Lord my strength" (Psalms 18:1), "I will call upon the Lord, who is worthy to be praised" (Psalms 18:3), "I will extol thee, O Lord" (Psalm 30:1), "I will bless the Lord at all times " (Psalms 34:1), "I will sing of mercy and judgment: unto thee, O Lord, I will sing" (Psalms101:1). "I will praise thee with my whole heart" (Psalms 138:1), "I will extol thee, my God, O King; and I will bless thy name for ever and ever" (Psalms 145:1).

I believe that He was expressing more than the fact that He was going to do. He was also expressing that He had a will to do, a deep desire to do. As a believer and disciple of Jesus Christ, we must will to be saved, will or desire to live saved, and we must be adamant or determined to stay saved.

Should one choose not to stay with God, these are some of the consequences for making that decision. God said, "Thou has forsaken me, saith the Lord, thou art gone backward: therefore will I stretch out my hand against thee, and destroy thee; I am weary with repenting" (Jeremiah 15:6).

"Again, when a righteous man doth turn from his righteousness, and commit iniquity, and I lay a stumbling block before him, he shall die because thou hast not given him warning. He shall die in his sin, and his righteousness which he hath done shall not be remembered; but his blood will I require at thine hand" (Ezekiel 3:20).

"If a man abide not in me, he is cast forth as a branch, and is withered; and men gather them, and cast them into the fire, and they are burned" (John 15:6).

"Howbeit then, when ye knew not God, ye did service unto them which by nature are no gods. But now, after that ye have known God, or rather are known of God, how turn ye again to the weak and beggarly elements, whereunto ye desire again to be in bondage? (Galatians 4:8, 9).

For if after they have escaped the pollution of the world through the knowledge of the Lord and Savior Jesus Christ, they are again entangled therein, and overcome, the latter end is worse with them than the beginning. "For it had been better for them not to have known the way of righteousness, than, after they hath known it, to turn from the holy commandment delivered unto them" (2 Peter 2:20, 21).

"Nevertheless, I have somewhat against thee, because thou hast left thy first love. Remember therefore from whence thou art fallen, and repent, and do the first works; or else I will come unto thee quickly, and will remove thy candlestick out of his pace, except thou repent" (Revelation 2:4, 5).

"And Jesus said unto him, no man, having put his hand to the plough, and looking back, is fit for the kingdom of God" (Luke 9:62).

God cannot lie, His word is true. I pray for the church that the Lord will bless and keep us always, as we continue to stay with Him.

As for me and mine, we're going to stay with the Lord!

CONCLUSION

Living life today has become more difficult than ever before in my lifetime. And as I look around, it appears to be equally so in the lives of people everywhere. But a life lived with God makes a life that is difficult, becomes easier to navigate through.

During these days of unrest in our country and abroad where seeds of discrimination, hatred, anger, and fear have been sown and we are witnessing the harvest of them, it is so expedient that we, who are believers, the Church, Christ's body, show forth Christ in our lives and in every area of our lives. So that in every place, as men go in and out throughout this world, they will see us, the Christian, radiating and displaying what it is like to live this life in God. Allowing all to see our good work and give our God the glory.

MY LIFETIME QUOTES

"You either believe God or you don't, there is nothing in between."

"If you can live it (the Christian life and the word), you can teach it with authority."

"Call yourself in check. If you check yourself, no one else will have to."

"The greatest witness that you will ever have is your walk (the way that you live) and not what you say."

"Choose to be happy (you can choose, it's your choice)."

"And I'm still in love with Jesus!"

"Preach and teach to bless, and never to impress."

ABOUT THE AUTHOR

Arthenia M. Newburn was born and raised in Hot Springs, Arkansas. She received salvation in 1975 and stands firm in the proclamation that she is still in love with Jesus. She is a member of the Bethel Missionary Baptist Church in Rockford, Illinois where Dr. Kerry L. Newburn is the pastor. She presently serves in many aspects of ministry and evangelism, preaching the gospel and speaking at various public events, conferences, and retreats. She is a wife of thirty-nine years, the mother of four, and a grandmother.

Made in the USA
Middletown, DE
14 September 2021

48339118R00033